In the name of God

***

Unwithering Flames: Book-6 "Shaheed Shayesteh Far; Narrated by His Wife" by: Aliyeh Sadat Hosseini
Copyright © 2023 Green Palm

All rights reserved. No portion of this book may be reproduced in any form without permission from the publisher. For permissions contact:
info@greenpalm.net
Translated and edited by: Green Palm books
Cover by Hussein Reza Vanaki
First Edition

To contribute towards future publications and be informed of the other books in the collection, please contact: info@Greenpalm.net

Unwithering Flames

— Book 6 - Hussein Shayesteh Far —

In order to have a fruitful and prosperous relationship, people have come to terms that they must love one another. Unfortunately, the meaning of true love has been lost. Many have relegated love to mere intimacy between a man and a woman. However, this is just the initial stage of true love, and we must aspire to reach a higher level beyond physical attraction. Such love is built on the foundation of honesty, enjoyment, selflessness, and spiritual attainment. Although many strive to reach this transcendent form of love, the affairs of this world become a barrier for them.

This series of books, entitled Unwithering Flames, recounts to us stories of those men and women who in the events of the Islamic Revolution and the Iraq's war against Iran turned away from this world just for the sake of God. In doing so, they became lovers in the true sense. They had the kind of love that did not just make the pain of this world bearable, rather it was something beautiful for them. The love whose flame has not dimmed even with martyrdom or death.

 www.GREENPALM.net
 +98 999 99 16 140
 info@GREENPALM.net

Hussein Shayesteh Far

Birth: November 8, 1953
Marriage to Razieh Bobash: August 24, 1987
Martyrdom: March 2, 2006

SYNOPSIS

You were craving for departure. Your feet wouldn't settle down on earth. Your eyes would dream about the blue sky. You knew you would finally meet with the light since you folded your impatience among your bodily pains. You remained patient. The pain would adorn you. The distance would make you fall into a deeper love. Your wounds would turn you into a mystic, and you would remain patient. To you, the earth was but a trifle. You were craving. You knew the sky was near, so near.

"Among the faithful are men who fulfill what they have pledged to Allah. Of them are some who have fulfilled their pledge, and of them are some who still wait, and they have not changed in the least." (Quran 33:23)

Contents

Chapter 1
A Soldier's Vow..9

Chapter 2
Hussein the Calmness of My Heart................25

Chapter 3
His Rani..37

Chapter 4
A Mother's Love..47

Chapter 5
Absence Makes the Heart Grow Fonder..........63

Chapter 6
Final Promises..79

Chapter 1

A Soldier's Vow

Mom sat next to me, she had something important to discuss.

"Mahmoud has put in a good word for him. About his gentlemanliness and his beliefs that match yours. He says he is a decent man and can count on him. But the rest is up to you, Razieh. You need to consider everything," she said.

Mahmoud was the son of my cousin Badrieh. He had known Hussein for almost a year, not to mention they had been together in several war operations. He used to speak a lot about his grit. "On the frontlines, he was the first to rush to the ammunition trucks to unload the boxes, while the Ba'athis[1] were firing." He was roughly aware of Hussein's injury and condition. He told my mom, "All these years, his kidney and bladder have not been functioning properly since thirteen flying shrapnel hit his head in one fell swoop. He can't walk well. He has seizures from time to time. In short, he doesn't have the healthiest body, but he is the right guy to spend a lifetime with."

As Mom finished speaking, I got cold feet. I was twenty-nine years old, and I did not want to consider marriage at that moment, but my old thoughts rejuvenated once more. They had become more like a dream. I was in my junior year studying nursing at Shahid Beheshti University.[2] But from the first year, I was dreaming about reaching the frontlines one way or another. I wanted to do something there. I wished to

---

1. Ba'athis are members and supporters of the Iraqi Arab Socialist Ba'ath party, which seized power in Iraq in the final decades of the twentieth century. The Iraqi war on Iran occurred during its reign led by Saddam Hussein.
2. Shahid Beheshti University (founded in 1959) is one of the biggest universities in Iran, located in Northern Tehran.

help the wounded soldiers with the skills I had learned in my nursing course. Perhaps, I couldn't do anything from a medical perspective, but washing their clothes was the least I could do. Mom refused. "Give up on going there; you know how unforgiving I can be at times!" she said. My mom wasn't always a strict woman. She wasn't used to giving us a straight-out no. She would offer some advice, but we were the ones to make the final decision, so when she became so rigid and said, "I don't want to hear about the frontline anymore," we all knew she wasn't going to change her mind, but with Mahmoud arriving and the way in which he described Hussein, I craved participating in the war once again.

Hussein came to the first few gatherings alone. He didn't even bring his mother. When I asked him why he was visiting without his mother, he responded, "I told her I want to decide first. Then, I will bring her." His father had passed away years ago. He was wearing a neat white suit the first time I saw him. While walking, he kept his hand against the wall and was dragging his feet. He also used to stutter a little. But none of these stood out like the front of his head, which had no hair. *A bad penny turns up everywhere; this is what I've always dreaded.*

A bald man! I told myself. I couldn't help it. I did not care about appearance, but I was sensitive to baldness. The dragging of his feet, the stuttering, even the hair loss were all the consequences of the shrapnel in his head. Later on, in his pre-injury photos, I saw a handsome young man with bushy black hair and a lovely face.

I wore my black *chador*[3] as usual. I was not used to wearing bright colors before *non-mahrams*.[4] Our rendezvous was at my cousin's home. I went upstairs with Mom, Badrieh, and Hussein. Like every other old building on Hashemi Street back then, their home had one room, a kitchen on the first floor and two rooms upstairs. They had designated the upper ones for serving guests. We were all sitting next to each other. Hussein was four years older than me. At the age of thirty-three, with glasses and a sunburnt face, he was like a mature and aged man. He was fluent in English and had an associate degree in Aviation

---

3. A *chador* is a long cloak-like garment, which covers the entire body, worn by Muslim women in Iran and some other countries in public places.

4. *Non-mahram* is every male person in front of whom a Muslim woman has to observe *hijab*.

Technology. He was twenty-seven when the war began and left everything behind to go to the frontline. He spoke slowly and with a slur, "When they refused to get me to the frontline on account of simply being an aviation technician, I joined Sepah[5] and along with my credentials, I was able to make it there. We were sent to the operational area from Hur Square barracks with the second expeditionary unit. Then, we joined Chamran's[6] Irregular Warfare Forces. May God bless his soul. I used to get along pretty well with Dr. Chamran," he said. When I observed him properly, I realized they looked so much alike. On our first gathering, Hussein told me about his routine, "I spend one week in Tehran, then I'm at the frontline for forty-five days. I've

---

5. Islamic Revolutionary Guard Corps, or Sepah, is a military and cultural organization, which was established about three months after the victory of the Islamic Revolution of Iran (in April 1979) under Imam Khomeini's advisement to protect the revolution and its achievements and to cooperate with the army of the Islamic Republic of Iran.

6. Mustafa Chamran is an Iranian physicist, politician, and commander who served as the first defense minister of Islamic Republic. He got martyred during the Iraq's war against Iran.

had the same routine from the beginning of the war. I wouldn't return for even that one week most of the times. I'm on a vow to be forty-five days at the frontlines and then stay home for one week, for as long as the war holds."

"What's the vow for?"

"I wasn't able to walk for months when I got injured. I was paralyzed. I couldn't even speak, just like a mute person. Doctors used to say sarcastically, 'Take him out of here. We cannot do anything for him. He doesn't walk, doesn't talk, and doesn't even hear anything.' But I heard them all. I just wasn't able to talk. One of my friends came to me one night, and we went to a prayer gathering to recite Du'a Kumayl.[7] There, I made a vow that I would reach the frontline in any way possible, just like the first days with forty-five days there, if my health recovered enough to at least write what I want. A while later, I was granted God's mercy. I could walk without a wheelchair. I

---

7. The supplication of Kumayl is a mystical supplication, which Imam 'Ali (a) taught Kumayl b. Ziyad, a close companion of his. It is commonly recited by Shias, particular on Thursday nights.

could say a few things. And now here I am after numerous medical interventions and speech therapy."

We went to Badrieh's home to talk another couple of times. We would all sit next to each other. I was too embarrassed to sit next to him alone. Hussein asked if I had any conditions for marriage.

"I just want to continue my studies. With a master's degree and doctorate considered, that would be roughly six more years of education. I want to complete that," I said.

"You can continue your studies as long as you wish. There's no problem with that." You could see the joy in my eyes. I adored what he said, as education was so crucial for me. He hit the bullseye by approving my request. I have had some pretty rough times with my studies. From my high school days to my time in the *hawza*[8] in Qom[9] and then

---

8. The Islamic seminary (*hawza 'ilmiyya*) is a religious educational institute, where its graduates are known as clerics.

9. Qom is the second most important pilgrimage city in Iran, where the mausoleum of Lady Ma'sumah (a), the daughter of Imam al-Kazim (a) and the sister of Imam al-Ridha (a) is located. The city has always been home to scholars and authorities.

studying nursing. I have some bittersweet memories from those days.

In the middle of the last year of high school, I came back home one day and said, "I won't go to school anymore." We used to live in Qaem Shahr[10] at that time, but my school was in Sari.[11] Schools in Qaem Shahr didn't hold mathematics courses. My older sister and I had to go to Sari and return home every day. A boy's school was attached to ours, with no wall separating the yards, only a metal fence. So, my mother sewed an extremely loose, long headscarf for me. I used to put it on in school, even during recess in the yard. Some kids used to make fun of me, "She must be bald that she covers herself so tightly," they would tease.

The school's headmaster was critical of the religious ones and those wearing *hijab*.[12] It was the year 1976. She was one of the

---

10. Qaem Shahr is a city in northern Iran. It is a tourist city located in Mazandaran Province.
11. Sari is the capital of Mazandaran Province.
12. The term *hijab* is mainly used to refer to a religious covering in the presence of *non-mahram* men. To maintain *hijab*, women must cover their body and adornments from *non-mahram* men.

few educational staff who was collaborating with the SAVAK.[13] She was hanged for treason after the revolution. One day, she came to the yard and suddenly removed my headscarf. The girls started to laugh. The boys were standing on the other side and kept staring at me. I put my hands on my head and sat on the ground. I didn't attend school anymore from that day onwards. *I'm not even going to go to university; so why should I finish school then?* I thought to myself. My mother did not approve, but she still wouldn't say anything. I did not dare tell my father. One day, he returned home at noon like never before. He thought I might be sick. When he came home unexpectedly a couple of times and saw me there, he questioned my mother.

"Why is she not at school?"

"She says that she isn't going to go to university. She wants to be a seminarian."

---

13. Intelligence and Security Organization of Country, abbreviated as SAVAK, was the security institute of the Pahlavi regime, which was founded in 1957 under the support and planning of the US, to enhance the monitoring of political dissidents and with the motto of "protecting the safety of the country."

Papa became mad and looked at me with fierce eyes.

"Papa, I want to go to Qom to study in the seminary. I'm more interested in this stuff. I want to know my religion by myself," I said.

"My daughter, you are good in your studies. That would be a pity. You can keep your beliefs in university, too. You can get to know them. You don't have to be a seminarian," he replied.

I was unlucky that my father had changed his mind. My older sister was also talented. She was craving to go to university. But Papa didn't like girls attending university back then. So, she had to go to the teacher education center instead. However, this time was different. My stubbornness wouldn't let me give up on my wish. I refused to take the final exams. When he found out I was serious about going to *hawza*, he said he would let me go to Qom, on the condition that I finish my studies and get my high school diploma. I began studying Mathematics, Geometry of Conics, and Mechanics at home. Each one was more dreadful than the other. I crammed all of them alone, without having a tutor. I wanted to graduate *summa cum*

laude. Despite all difficulties, I passed the exams and ranked first among those sitting for re-examination. Papa kept his promise, and we set off for Qom with my mom.

We did not know anyone there, except for a cleric, Mr. Mohaghegh, who was one of our relatives. He was a great help. He introduced us to the seminary, where we were supposed to register. Then, he assisted us in finding a place to rent. The landlord was a pious man. The building was old. He was living on one side of the yard, and on the other, there was a room, kitchen, and an exclusive bath and toilet for the tenant. My mother stayed with me for one week. We agreed that my grandmother would come to Qom to live with me. Despite being seventy-years old, she was full of life. She would do the shopping and cooking all by herself. And all I did was study. One month after the beginning of the school year, I entered Mr. Ghoddosi's seminary. I faced lots of ups and downs in those five or six years following the revolution and the beginning of the war, when I was residing in Qom, studying. It was challenging but not void of sweet moments. I started to study experimental sciences in 1982. I took the university entrance exam, was accepted for the nursing degree, and returned to Tehran. Studying had permeated into my being and had become second nature to me.

During our proposal meetings, Hussein told me his chances of fertility were next to none due to his injuries. I wasn't expecting this. I might have accepted other conditions, but giving up on having a child was not an easy pill to swallow. Hussein narrated the story of him being injured in great detail.

"It was the Operation Fath-ol-Mobin.[14] The Ba'athi had counter-attacked, capturing a part of the area. One of their tanks approached us in the middle of the rain of bullets. I grasped an RPG-7 and moved forward. I was only ten to fifteen meters away from the tank, when I shot it. I couldn't understand anything afterward. I heard the rest of the story from others. My cousin was in the same operation. He assumed I had been martyred when he saw me lying on the ground with shrapnel in my face. The explosion had torn off a part of my skull, and I was bleeding profusely. He was certain that

---

14. Operation Fath-ol-Mobin was a successful operation carried out by Iranian soldiers in 1982 against the invading Ba'athi occupiers.

I was dead, and so he removed my tag and retreated with the others. The Iraqis skipped me while administering the *coup de grace* for the half-dead wounded soldiers. They assumed I had already perished. Twenty-four hours later, our soldiers recaptured the area. The Ba'athis retreated. The soldiers gathered the wounded Iraqis to transfer them to the hospital. I was mistaken for one of the Iraqis, since my skin color was dark, too. They sent me back with them to a hospital in Isfahan.[15] I was admitted there for four months. I couldn't walk. I wasn't able to say that I was Iranian, and not Iraqi. My cousin had handed my tag over to the IRGC and told my family that I'd been martyred. They held a funeral and hung a big picture of me on the wall. Until one day, they broadcasted a TV program recorded in our hospital. They showed the wounded on TV. My nephew Ali, who was nine, recognized me. He told my sister, 'I saw uncle Hussein on TV. He was in the hospital. His head was bandaged.' My sister didn't believe him. She assumed the kid was making up a story. But Ali insisted on his words so much that it

---

15. Isfahan is one of the largest historic cities of Iran and the Islamic civilization.

moved my sister. She started searching for me in Tehran hospitals. 'We don't have such a person here. But there are some wounded soldiers with unknown identities in Isfahan. Pay a visit there, too,' she was told. Zahra came to Isfahan. At the hospital, when I saw her, I just rapidly punched my chest, so that she might possibly recognize me. I wasn't able to shout, 'It's me, Hussein; your brother.' She finally noticed me and came over to me. She was crying in shock. She told the story to my mother, bit by bit. My mom fell ill. 'You want to dredge up the past. I was getting used to this pain,' she sobbed. They transferred me to Labbafinezhad Hospital in Tehran. It took me a few months to be able to move my lips and stutter a few words. Then, I realized my kidney and bladder were not working well and that I might never have children."

I took Hussein's medical file to Labbafinezhad Hospital. We used to go there frequently for our college courses. It was a hospital for medical students, so I knew some physicians there. Dr. Sim Foroush, Hussein's urologist, was also working there. He recognized Hussein when I showed him the files. He was aware of Hussein's condition.

He emphasized that it was unlikely that Hussein could have children. I showed the file to another doctor. Dr. Ghiasvand had just come back from the United States and had a Ph.D. in Genetics. He made the same diagnosis as Dr. Sim Foroush. I was certain that living with Hussein would be full of difficulties. But deep down in my heart, I knew I wanted him. "Not having children might not be a problem at all. I can take care of him with ease of mind." I could not let go of the thought of how much joy serving a veteran would bring to me.

Chapter 2

Hussein the Calmness of My Heart

I was young and I was craving to fight and work on the frontlines. I had been aching for this since I was a teenager. This spirit might might have been rooted in my brother's deeds. He was three years older than me. Back in 1969-1970, when I was twelve, and he was fifteen, our hobby was buying books rather than playing outside or going to the movies. We loved reading books. We would combine our allowances to buy some books, including: books about the history of Iran, France, and Russia, poetry, fiction, religion, even Marxist ones.

Ali used to receive forbidden books from his teacher. They were a crime to hold, like the works of Muhammad Reza Hakimi.[16] Later on, his teacher was martyred in the turmoil of the revolution. Ali would say, "Razieh! You should listen to *Mihan Parastan Radio* every day. Buy a notebook and keep note of the important sayings. But let no one see your notes!" *Mihan Parastan Radio* was an anti-regime radio network that belonged to the Fedai Guerrilla Organization,[17] and it was on air from Baghdad. I bought a notebook and stuck some pictures on the notes, so they wouldn't be apparent. Ali, despite his young age, was the one who taught me the concepts of "tyrant", "tyranny", and "fighting". Later, my thoughts deepened in the seminary.

In 1978 when the protests were raging in Qom, we could not reach the streets easily. One day, from the corner of the seminary window, I witnessed the army forces shooting and killing clerics and ordinary people with armored tanks near Ahanchi

---

16. Muhammad Reza Hakimi (d. 2021), a prominent Iranian Islamic scholar, and religious thinker who has numerous works in his career.

17. The Organization of Iranian People's Fedai Guerrillas, simply known as Fadaiyan-e Khalq was an underground Marxist–Leninist guerrilla organization in Iran.

Bridge. Up until the revolution, we were distributing influential manifestos[18] here and there. We would receive the handouts from Mr. Ghoddosi, the head of the seminary. I was a diligent student and the headmaster was counting on me. In the summer of 1978, I went to Fasa[19] as a clergywoman for preaching. Mr. Ghoddosi handed me the latest pamphlets from Imam Khomeini that were sent from France to distribute in Fasa. I held meetings there to talk to my peers. Then the war began, and I was aching for the warfronts.

Marrying Hussein could calm my heart, but my father was not content. He already liked Hussein, but he was nervous for me.

"You'll get into trouble, Razieh. Would you be able to handle that?" he asked.

---

18. Since November 1964 to February 1979, the Pahlavi regime exiled Imam Khomeini to Iraq and then France. During this period, he issued manifestos in which he expressed his position and led people's campaigns against the Pahlavi regime. The Pahlavi regime had criminalized any duplication or distribution of Imam Khomeini's manifestos.

19. Fasa is an ancient populated city in Fars province, located fifty kilometers in the southeast of Shiraz.

I wasn't confident either. But I became more determined after having a couple of dreams following those get-togethers with Hussein. I dreamed of being in a vast place packed with chairs, as though someone was about to give a speech. As I listened carefully, I heard Shaheed Ghoddosi's voice, the seminary headmaster when I was a student, who had been martyred after the revolution. It was his voice but within Hussein's visage. I ran to him, but the guards stopped me. "It's me, Bobash," I shouted. He recognized me and we greeted each other. He started to walk, and I kept following him. I was putting my feet in his footsteps. I dreamed the same thing several different times, feeling weird after waking up, as if my life was about following in Hussein's footsteps. I made myself confident by consulting the holy Quran *(istikhara)*.[20] I asked my cousin to inform him, "My answer is yes."

The whole family was shocked. "Razieh must be insane. She'll be doomed," my uncle said. Papa was still worried. Mom remained

---

20. *Istikhara* is to tell fortunes or seeking counsel from the Quran. Some Muslims perform *istikhara* when they doubt about a decision, and by virtue of Quranic verses, they ask for God's guidance.

silent, but I'd already decided to take a leap of faith and marry with Hussein.

The next time Hussein and his mother came to our house, it was a more formal meeting than the previous ones. They came over bringing a bouquet and confection. My father was also there. Hussein and I were almost done talking; the elders were chatting. Hussein's mom was from Saveh;[21] she was a *sayyideh*.[22] "All my children are *sayyids*,[23] too. They might not have a family tree, but their late father and all his ancestors were born in the Sadat neighborhood in Yazd,"[24] she said. It didn't matter to me. I valued him as a son of the Prophet (s) as he was a *sayyid* on his mother's side; I kept the same respect throughout our time together. His mother sat next to me and said quietly, "I hope you are not a Turk. Hussein is not very willing to marry a Turk, because of their unique traditions." *Poor Hussein, What an unlucky guy*, I laughed in my heart.

---

21. Saveh is a city in Markazi Province of Iran. It is located about 100 km southwest of Tehran.
22. A female descendant of Prophet Muhammad (s).
23. A male descendant of Prophet Muhammad (s).
24. Yazd is the capital of Yazd Province, Iran. The city is located 270 km southeast of Isfahan.

We were Turks, but you couldn't guess that from our accent. Even Mahmoud, my aunt's grandson, a friend of Hussein's, couldn't say a word in Turkish. That's why Hussein had not noticed we were Turks. My father was born in Makhachkala, Soviet Union. My grandfather was of Iranian origin, and married a Shi'ite Russian woman in Russia. Before the Second World War began, the Soviet Union expelled the foreigners from their territory. He returned to Iran with his wife and three children. My father was the middle child, and he was nine at that point. Six months after their arrival, his mother got food poisoning and died. My grandfather also died of grief over his wife a couple of months later. My older uncle took the responsibility of the family. Living in Iran was challenging, as my father's first language was Russian. Later, when my parents met and married, my mother taught him most of what he knew of Persian. We used to call him "Papa". Apart from Persian, he also learned many Islamic principles and beliefs from my mother. My mom was the granddaughter of one of the greatest *mujtahids*[25] of Tabriz.[26] They migrated to Qaem Shahr, Mazandaran, for her father's job in the railway. Years later, my parents met in Qaem Shahr, and married there. My siblings and I were born in the same city.

The elders finished talking and decided we would marry a couple of months later. Hussein used to send me pictures and letters when he was on the frontline. He was good at writing. His letters were replete with passion he had. He would also compose poetry. I would miss him and would send him letters from time to time. We still had not come out of our shells. Being *non-mahrams* had also made us more comfortable writing, rather than talking. We married on August 24, 1987. We decided to hold a small, intimate ceremony, as we were not used to squandering. I knew Hussein was short of money. Hussein had been working and studying since his father passed away, when he was seventeen. His mom would always compliment and praise him for this. .

---

25. *Mujtahid* or *faqīh* is a person who has the ability to deduce the jurisprudential *(fiqhi)* rulings from reliable sources.
26. Tabriz is a city in the northwest of Iran and the capital city of East Azerbaijan province.

"Their late father had rented a junk shop near Edam Square. When he passed away, he hadn't left us anything. Hussein was a sixth-grade student of mathematics then, but he had to change his major to Experimental Sciences to have spare time to work. He had tried many jobs, from street peddling to welding and selling newspapers. He would spend all his money on his family. He had younger siblings to look after. He provided his sister's dowry and married her off. He also paid for one of his brother's wedding ceremonies. Then he went to the warfront," his mother shared.

Hussein wasn't unwilling to see me in a wedding dress and hold an exceptional ceremony, but I didn't agree to it. I didn't want to be saddled with debt from the early days of our marriage. We didn't buy anything for the ceremony. Only one day, he picked me up to buy a ring for 450 tomans.[27]

There was no one in the marriage registry bureau on the day of the wedding except for Papa, Mom, myself, and Hussein, along with his mother. He was wearing the same white suit he had worn during the proposal meeting.

---

27. *Toman* is the Iranian currency.

"How much is the agreed *mahr*[28] of the bride?" *Aqed*[29] asked Hussein.

"Whatever she demands," Hussein replied.

We had not talked about this earlier, but I had told Papa that the number forty was my favorite. "Forty Bahar Azadi Coins.[30] Do you agree?" Papa asked Hussein. Hussein consented. We had the wedding vow with the mentioned *mahr* and a volume of the Quran, and then I became his wife. We spent the next couple of hours in my parents' home. We had rented a wedding venue in Salsabil Street, and invited only some close relatives. After the wedding dinner, we returned home again. Hussein had three or four days off. My parents left the house, so we could be comfortable. They had gone to stay at my cousin's home. Hussein had lived alone for a couple of years since his injury. The Organization of

---

28. *Mahr* is the money paid or owed by the groom to the bride at the time of marriage.
29. Persons authorized to solemnize marriage in Islam are called *aqed*.
30. Bahar Azadi Coin is Iranian gold coins.

Veterans and Martyrs[31] had provided him a home in Shemiran.[32] He was alone there. His mother and siblings would visit him on the weekends.

I went to the kitchen to prepare some breakfast when I got up in the morning. My mother had packed the refrigerator with food for us to have something to eat for several days. "Hussein, do you want to have breakfast?" I asked.

He shook his head. *He's not into breakfast*, I assumed. I made something for myself and ate in the kitchen. I asked him again a couple of minutes later.

"What will you have for lunch?"

Averting his eyes from the book, he looked at me.

"Nothing, I have no appetite."

---

31. The Organization of Martyrs and Veterans is a governmental institution that was established after the victory of the Islamic Revolution in Iran at the command of Imam Khomeini to support veterans, those injured in the war, and families of martyrs in Iran.

32. Shemiran is an area in the north of Tehran.

I was tickled pink. I thought this man came from heaven. I hated cooking so much. *Thank God he doesn't care about food.* I used to escape from cooking. Even in the seminary, I would substitute my cooking rotation for cleaning the toilets and mopping the corridors. It never crossed my mind that he might be too shy to ask for food. I wasn't a stand on ceremonies type, I would eat alone, but he didn't have a single bite. Only occasionally he would drink some tea. I thought he might be abstemious, one of those types who eat and sleep little. *That must be why he's so thin*, I guessed. However, after a couple of days, I saw him having a bite or two. I realized timidity was behind all that abstinence. When we broke the ice between us a little, he spoke to me about it.

"My goodness! I was just too shy to ask you for food, I thought I would starve to death, if I didn't ask."

I felt embarrassed, but I also burst into laughter. To make me less upset, Hussein told me a story from his time at the frontline.

"Well, I should say I'm good at bearing hunger. Once on the frontline, we had to survive in a swamp for three days with a single pipe to breathe. There was no water or food."

When I got to know him better, I found out he had a very courteous nature. He wouldn't even eat when we had guests. He was reticent and wasn't used to talking about his past or himself. He also wouldn't tell much when he returned from the warfront. I would struggle to draw something out of him. But you couldn't miss his humor. His words were full of cheer and affection. I never felt bored around him. I liked his manners, and I became more and more interested in him with each passing day. Hussein's time off ended so soon. I knew it was time for him to leave. We were supposed to be apart for forty-five days. I was heartbroken. Early in the morning, Mojtaba Sinjali came to pick Hussein up with his motorcycle. They were going to the frontlines. It was always this friend of his who would pick him up. I would stand still near the door and watch him leave, until I could barely see him anymore. Not only the first time, but I would also do it time and again. Once when he was back from the warfront, I spoke to him about how he used to leave.

"You're mean! You won't even turn back to look at me when you're on the bike."

"If I did so, I wouldn't be able to leave you."

Chapter 3

His Rani

We lived for nine months with my parents. Everyone cherished him, as he was so courteous. Even my uncle grew fond of his character. I would study, and I was a sessional instructor of Arabic and Theology. Finally, we managed to rent the first floor of a building, which belonged to Mr. Farsijani, a friend and a fellow soldier of Hussein. I did not give in to living in Shemiran. I felt so alienated there. I asked Hussein to return the house to the Organization of Veterans and Martyrs, so we could rent somewhere near my parents' home. Farsijani's place was on Khoush Street. It was old, but a positive factor was that we could finally live independently, and the landlord was Mr. Farsijani's mother. We had the first floor, with two adjoining rooms. A kitchen, a toilet, and a bath were in the yard. Farsijani's mother was a righteous, and kind woman.

Hussein followed his routine of forty-five days at the frontline and one week at home. They would send him back if he fell sick. When they would find out he was a war veteran, they wouldn't dispatch him again. Hussein, however, was not giving up and would get the dispatch approval from a different base. Of course, he could not reach the place where the fighting was taking place; he would only do occupational service. He did this until the war finished. Operation Mersad[33] was one of his greatest regrets. He couldn't participate in it because of his urological problems; It was the only one he ever missed. In each one of those forty-five-day intervals, he suffered several injuries. Once, the shrapnel hit him near his spinal cord. His injuries kept increasing.

He used to call me "Rani".

---

33. Operation Mersad was a large-scale operation by Iranian soldiers in 1988 against the forces of the terrorist People's Mojahedin Organization of Iran (MEK), known as Monafeghin. The operation was planned and commanded by Shaheed Sayyad Shirazi.

"Everyone calls me Razi. What's this Rani thing about?" I asked. He would only laugh. It took several months until he revealed the secret.

"It means 'Razieh, my sweetheart.' I made it up myself. It's pretty."

He would call me Rani until the last days leading up to his martyrdom. I was petrified when he had seizures for the first time. I forgot everything I had learned at university about symptoms of seizures or when they occur. I was baffled. He had just come back from the warfront. He went to take a shower and trim his beard as usual, but a couple of hours later, he began trembling and fell to the ground. He was rolling around the room whilst biting his tongue. Blood oozed from his mouth. He calmed down for a couple of minutes. I was confused about what to do, and then he started to tremble once more. He had five or six seizures in a row until the scary trembling ceased. He fell asleep exhausted.

Later, I learned what to do. Whenever Hussein was staring at a certain point, he would have hysteria. I would rush to get a sheet, roll it up and put it between his teeth, so he was unable to bite his tongue. I would prepare his drugs. After the seizures and before he woke up, I would tidy up the room, so he wouldn't notice anything. He wouldn't remember a thing.

His dentures remained a secret until I saw them, while trying to keep his mouth open. I liked the gap in his teeth. I would tell him, "Hussein, I love your teeth diastema." Embarrassed, he would close his mouth immediately. He didn't want me to stare at them. Upon finding out his dentures were revealed to me, he became so upset. A blow of shrapnel had broken most of his teeth. From that point, he was forced to wear dentures. I never understood why he was so touchy about them. "I won't forgive you if anyone finds out about this," he would say in a seriocomic tone.

"It's not a big deal. Everyone will end up using those," I said with laughter.

The war ended, and Hussein remained nostalgic about those days. Sometimes, he would stay in the room staring at the photos taken at the warfront. He would keep himself busy by listening to the radio. Despite having difficulty walking, he would do most of the shopping himself and help me with the housework. When he wasn't well, I didn't expect him to do anything. For a while, the Organization of Veterans and Martyrs found him a job in a clinic. They would even send a car to drive him there, but his career didn't last long as his seizures intensified by meeting other veterans there. He also smashed the glasses once or twice. He left the clinic a month later.

Occasionally, his war-time friends would visit him, and take him out for a drive. That would change his mood. One night, Mr. Farsijani came to our home. I offered them tea and fruit and left the room. An hour later, no sounds were coming out of the room. I listened carefully; nothing but someone wheezing. I rushed to the room.

"Dear Lord! Hussein, what are you doing?"

He had put his arms around his friend, squeezing his neck. Farsijani went blue, with his eyes ready to pop out. He was suffocating.

"Hussein, let go of him."

He looked at me with fierce eyes.

"Ba'athi! Ba'athi!"

"He's not Ba'athi, Hussein. It's Mr. Farsijani. Let him go."

Farsijani's face was getting bluer. Hussein loosened his arms for a moment, which allowed his friend to rush out of the house.

I was gradually giving up on getting my master's degree. I had to forget about it; Hussein needed more care. Mrs. Farsijani also let us know that she would need the house for her newly-married son, so we had to vacate the house. Hussein asked the Organization of Veterans and Martyrs for a place. They gave us a house on Enghelab Street, opposite the University of Tehran. One of those post-revolution confiscated houses, that were older than Mr. Farsijani's building. It seemed like it had survived the Second World War. There was a hall downstairs; the toilet was seven or eight steps up, and you needed to climb a couple more steps to reach two rooms. Hussein had difficulty walking up the stairs, so we had a plasterer make a small room on the lower level, so he could rest and make himself comfortable.

I wished I could show our kids to the doctors, who had told us we couldn't have children. I wanted to show them Zahra, Zeynab, and Amir Hussein and say, "The will of God is above everything else."

I often saw him crying and asking for a child in his prayers. I'd never seen him cry except for the grief of Imam al-Husayn (a).[34]

"Are you a kid now? Why are you crying like this?" I would tell him.

"This is my only wish. To have a son who could do what I never did for you. I want him to help you when he grows up." I wanted to bear his child, too. I would risk all difficulties just to see his children playing in this house. His prayers had been answered soon after. We went to Dr. Sim Fourosh for Hussein's monthly check-up with a twenty-day infant. He took a look at the kid with surprise.

"This is a miracle. If not, it's just a one-time gift. It can't happen again."

I had the most difficult days of my life when I was pregnant. Each one of my pregnancies had its problems. But the sounds of their laughter would let the flower

---

34. Imam al-Husayn (a) the third Shiite Imam, was the son of Imam 'Ali b. Abi Talib (a) and Lady Fatima al-Zahra (a).

of hope blossom in my being. For our first child, Hussein got the test results himself. He came back with a box of confections. I stood up.

"What is it? Positive?"

He nodded with laughter. I couldn't believe my eyes. Although I knew having a baby meant I needed to forget about continuing my education, I was so thrilled that I couldn't care less about that. My parents had moved to Qaem Shahr. Mom couldn't come over much, because of my younger siblings. Hussein would help me with the housework, although I didn't want him to carry out my duties. Sometimes, he'd like to wash the dishes or make one of his special omelets, those he used to make on the warfront, with dates and onions. Hussein wasn't a picky eater; he would consume anything. All he would ask for was the table to be neatly arranged. Even if we had no more than some water, he would like me to pour it into a pretty pitcher and place it on the table.

Hussein was so generous. He would donate as much money as he could afford. He took us to a fancy restaurant on a road called Vali-e Asr Street one night. We took a cab. When the car was stuck in heavy traffic, when he opened the door and ran to the other side of the road to give some money to a poor man sitting on the sidewalk.

Chapter 4

A Mother's Love

Everyone was expecting a boy from my second pregnancy. I was too, but Hussein remained quiet, as if he knew everything. We were facing more pressure. I had to take care of my first daughter, Zahra, and bear the pregnancy. In addition, Hussein was not feeling well; the number of his seizures had increased, and his bladder had almost stopped functioning. Doctors believed he needed surgery. We took him to the hospital to perform a cystoplasty. They removed thirty-five centimeters of his small intestine during the surgery and implanted an artificial bladder in his body. We brought him home. We couldn't afford the cost of living anymore, especially with Hussein's medication. So, I decided to find a job. I knew some people in the Department of Education of Tehran's District Ten. I found sessional employment in a school with their help. My mother used to look after Hussein and Zahra, and in the meantime, I would teach Arabic at school.

I was alone when my labor pain started. My mom was in Gachsaran[35] for my sister's delivery. My baby was born prematurely in my eighth month. Work pressure could have been the cause. I went to the hospital and returned home in agony for three days and nights. I would squeeze my fingers in pain so as not to scream. On the third night, Hussein called his mother. We took Zahra and went to Najmieh hospital. There, the chief physician was a friend of Hussein's. He let us stay in the prayer room.

"Rest here tonight. Doctors have found your condition to be critical."

Zahra was feeling drained. Hussein and his mom stayed a bit longer and then returned home. The baby, a girl, was born at midnight. They put the baby in the NICU.

---

35. Gachsaran County is in Kohgiluyeh and Boyer-Ahmad province, southwest of Iran.

Hussein called the hospital at 6 o'clock in the morning, intending to speak with me.

"I called the hospital at four, asking them to connect me to your room. I wanted to talk. I told them I knew the baby was born. They said it wasn't possible. Rani, I dreamed the baby was born. A girl, right?"

"Yeah, it's a girl. But they won't let us see her just yet."

On the third day, they handed us our little girl, and we returned home. A couple of days later, my mother came to Tehran. She asked to name the girl "Narges" after Imam Zaman's mother, Hussein also liked the name, because the baby was born on the same night on the birthday of Imam Zaman (a).[36] But we also had "Zeynab" and "Fatemeh" as options. They were Hussein's mother's suggestions. We wrote down the names and picked one by chance. "Zeynab" was drawn three consecutive times.

Some months later, we traveled to my sister's place in a northern town to change

---

36. Mid-Sha'ban (Sha'ban 15th) is the birthday of Imam al-Mahdi (a), the twelfth Shiite Imam, whom Shias believe to be the promised savior. Mid-Sha'ban celebrations are among the biggest Shiite ceremonies.

Hussein's mood. That was the second trip I had with Hussein. The previous year, the Organization of Veterans and Martyrs sent us on a trip to Mashhad.[37] The weather was favorable, so it raised our spirits. Hussein couldn't resist the water. He was a butterfly stroke instructor, holding a coaching license. Despite undergoing cystoplasty, he dived into the sea. He kept swimming forward while I yelled at him.

"Don't go any further, for God's sake."

He went too far to be seen. My brother-in-law took a boat to the middle of the sea to bring him back.

By the following February, we had our only son. The third pregnancy was bittersweet. I dared the coming days, as I had to stop working. I thought to myself, *how am I going to raise three children all alone?* Despite all the problems, Hussein's presence would encourage me.

---

37. Mashhad is a city in northeastern Iran, located in the center of Razavi Khorasan Province. The city is home to the mausoleum of Imam al-Ridha (a), the eighth Shiite Imam.

"Razieh, stop crying, for God's sake! Don't be upset! Let God bestow us with this child. I know this one is the boy I wished for. He'll be a great help for you."

Reciting the Quran was the only thing calming my soul in that time of hardship.

There was a fruit store adjacent to our house. The owner was also a war veteran. Hussein would socialize with him occasionally. Talking together would brighten up his days; besides, it was the only place he could go for a stroll. At other times, I wouldn't let him stay alone in his room for too long. Once, he was incredibly emotional and I saw him burning his old war-time photos. I ran to save the images; they were valuable memories. Despite these emotional outbursts, he would always find a way to cheer me up. He would crack some jokes when I was feeling distraught. He would keep making faces until I forgot all about my exhaustion and misery and crack a smile. His stuttering increased. I was the only one who could understand his words, like an infant who no one could understand except their mother.

I was five months pregnant when a horrible incident happened. I was upstairs with Zahra and Zeynab praying, when Hussein came up to join us. He lost his balance and fell down the stairs. I never knew if it was the shrapnel in his head having moved or if something else had taken place. His condition kept worsening from that night on. He was no longer the person he used to be. He had to receive permanent catheterization. He would also lose his consciousness frequently which would bring about a dangerous situation, if I was distracted from him. I had to be watchful of the cigarettes in his hand just in case he would fall asleep and drop them on the blanket and set the whole place on fire. I had to leave the kids alone for some moments to do the shopping, only when he was asleep. I couldn't sleep at night, as I was worried that he would stand on his feet and fall again or have seizures. I did not sleep a wink for eight nights. Bearing a baby in me, sometimes, I would feel I was about to die from the weariness. I was inches away from giving up when the house bell rang at sunset. My mom was standing behind the door. My savior angel! She frowned when she saw the three of us like that.

"I had a hunch you're not doing well. I came to Tehran to stay for a while."

"You just take care of Hussein and the kids, Mom. I need to sleep for a couple of hours."

"I'll handle this. Rest up."

It felt like a brief nap as I woke up. Mom approached me.

"So, you're finally awake? Do you know how long you slept? It's been about two days now. You wouldn't even open your eyes for your meal and prayers."

She stayed until Muhammad Hussein was born. When my labor began, I put my clothes on and headed toward the hospital alone. My mother had to spend the night looking after Hussein and the girls. In the wake of my checkup, the doctor made a decision.

"The baby's condition is not proper. You will need to have a cesarean."

"I can't. My husband is a battle-scarred veteran. He's not feeling well. I need to take care of him myself. There's no one to help me. If I undergo the operation, I can't even see to myself, let alone Hussein."

I returned home. The pain was so much that I thought I wouldn't make it out alive. I drew up my will and put it in an envelope. I told my mother to tear it open if I didn't return home.

I went to the hospital again the next day, but I heard the same response.

"You will need to have a cesarean."

I returned home. I followed the same routine for the next eleven days, hoping for a normal delivery. I was ailing on the last day. They didn't let me out. The doctor came to me shouting at the nurses.

"You are killing my patient. Why isn't she in the operating room?"

"She didn't consent. And there is no one accompanying her," the nurses replied.

"She is insane. I can't hear the fetal heartbeat. Her blood pressure has dropped too. Prepare the room for surgery," the doctor shouted.

I was half-conscious. When the baby was born, I heard the nurses.

"She already has two daughters, and they're given a son now."

I ascertained the baby was a boy. I was blissful, mainly for Hussein. Having a son was what he had always wished for. I couldn't see the baby for a couple of days. I wasn't feeling good, either. When I recuperated, they brought me a tanned, bulky boy. The hospital discharged me, and my younger brother picked us up.

When we got home, I handed the child over to Hussein.

"Finally, what should we call him?"

Before he was born, Hussein used to say, "I know the baby is a boy. I'll name him Abolfazl." I said, "But I like Muhammad Hussein. Abolfazl is a nice name, too. But it reminds me of my three uncles whose names were Abolfazl, and they all died at an early age." However, Hussein did not buy into it. He kept telling me "His name is Abolfazl. Just saying," until the very last moment I was going to the hospital. However, it seemed like he felt pity for all the pain I endured when he looked at the baby and laughed.

"Let's call him Muhammad Hussein."

A few months later, Mom had a word with me.

"You can't keep up this situation anymore. You sold all your gold, but there are still some debts. You should go to work while you're still young and capable."

"Where should I leave my three children? Hussein himself is no better than a kid. He needs care."

"Find a job. I promise to take care of them."

In early 1991, I continued my teaching career. The Department of Education regarded my former activities as a sessional teacher for those few months and officially employed me. That was the best opportunity I needed at that moment. I used to go to school twice a week, two shifts in a row, from morning until noon. Mom would stay with Hussein and the kids.

Looking at Hussein would strengthen my motivation. I would look at his feeble body, which was emaciating. I thought to myself, *this man is in a world of pain, but never regrets anything. So why should I?* He had a saying about this, "I'll make yearning long for me to give up. I sacrificed everything for my cause, and I won't stop now." He kept getting weaker, but in my eyes, he was more precious than ever. I might have given up if he had complained, but he never did. Through the pain of his body and soul, he taught me patience.

I had enjoyed a prosperous childhood in Papa's house. I used to pretend to be asleep at night until I was twelve, so my father would come and kiss me, lift me, and put me on my bed. Mom would never let us run out of school accessories, not for a single day. Now, how is such a pampered girl tolerating these challenging days so lovingly? It was a divine trial. It was the time to exercise all those theoretical courses learned in the seminary, and apply them in my life. In the same year, the Organization of Veterans and Martyrs informed us that a medical commission was needed to reevaluate the severity of a veteran's injury every five years.

"You should bring all of his medical files, or his case will be closed in the Organization of Veterans and Martyrs, and you won't receive any more services," they said.

After the school year, I went in search of the files. The first hospital was Labbafinezhad. I knew they had transferred Hussein there from Isfahan, when he was injured. But I had no clue about any other places where he had been hospitalized. I had to inquire at other hospitals. In Labbafinezhad, they told me, "We've transferred the old files to the archive room to register the data in our database. We usually dispose of any file from ten years ago. It won't be easy finding yours."

"I had my nursing internship here. We are colleagues in a sense, and this file holds great importance for me," I said.

I kept going there for a week, but it was of no use. The head of the Archives Department seemed to be bored of my persistence.

"Ma'am, go search for your documents among the files yourself. See what you can find," he said.

I remained speechless when they opened the door. A room stuffed with files and ledger binders up to the ceiling. *They have every right to avoid this room*, I thought. Deep in my heart, I pleaded with Imam Zaman to help me find the file. "O, Hojjat ibn al-Hassan,[38] assist me. For my childrens'

---

38. Hojjat b. al-Hassan is one of the titles of Imam al-Mahdi, the twelfth Shiite Imam who is in occultation,

sake," I prayed. I put my hand on a file and pulled it out. Tears welled up in my eyes. It was Hussein's. They had filed up most of the documents showing the severity of his injury there. Other hospitals either didn't have the files or were insignificant except for Sorkhe Hesar, which held Hussein's psychiatry files. When studying the file, I found out a brain injury had critically damaged his nerves. He was admitted to the hospital four times for getting shell-shocked. The committee had evaluated his shock rate as forty-five percent; it was not trivial. I took the files to the department to arrange a medical commission. "The veteran himself should be present, too," they said.

Hussein wouldn't listen. I persuaded him after a great deal of effort. Dozens of doctors gathered around him for an hour, prying him with questions, but they didn't arrive at a decision that day, as some of them were in disagreement. I had to take him for another session. He wouldn't budge to go there at all. But no matter how hard I tried, he disagreed, "Hussein, look how hard I've tried to get us here so far. Just come this

---

and the Shias wait for his reappearance.

one time." I made an excuse to get him out of the house. The Medical Commission Center was on Qarani Street. We got out of the car at the intersection of Taleqani and Qarani Streets. He suddenly recognized the place. He realized I was taking him to the commission meeting, he was outraged, and began to beat me on the sidewalk. People had gathered and they were about to thrash him; but I shouted, "You stay out of this. He can't help himself. He's in a postictal aggressive state. It'll be over in a moment." A while later, he sat down on the sidewalk. When he simmered down, he consented to attend the commission meeting; out of pity, perhaps. "Finish the case today. I can't bring him here anymore," I told the commission's members. Finally, they gave us the results; they approved a seventy-percent injury.

With every passing day, a part of the house would collapse. One day, I heard Zeynab screaming while I was tending to Hussein. I ran to the corridor to see a massive pit of one-and-a-half-meter width and almost two-meter depth along the stairs. Zeynab had fallen into the pit shrieking, with her face covered with dust. I pulled her out and removed the dirt from her clothes. I called the Organization of

Veterans and Martyrs right away. I had done that previously and asked them to inspect the house themselves, but they had kept postponing it. My father filled the pit with a barrel and some bricks. But it was no place to live anymore. My old friend, Mrs. Hamiz, came to the rescue. I knew her from the seminary; they would pay us a visit frequently, as well. Her husband, Mr. Haeri, was the Deputy Minister of Defense and a friend of Mr. Rafigh Doost, the head of the Organization of Veterans and Martyrs. They had gone to the Organization of Veterans and Martyrs and clarified our living conditions. Hamiz came to me and said, "The office has agreed to provide you with a grant of three million tomans, so that you can buy a house." That much was not sufficient, but I was able to make do with it. I left no stone unturned, searching for a modest house in District Ten, until I found a five million toman house. I borrowed one and a half million from my father, and we moved to our new place. We modified and repaired it.

Chapter 5

Absence Makes the Heart Grow Fonder

In 1993, Hussein's physical condition worsened. He had to receive catheterization four times a day. I was lucky I had studied nursing, which was a great help. Zahra and Zeynab were older, and they used to play together. Muhammad Hussein however, was younger, and he was a bit of a handful. He started toddling so soon. I had no choice but to tie him to a dresser, with a piece of fabric, so he wouldn't fall down the stairs. I had to be all eyes while taking care of Hussein. He could not be tied up like a kid. I had to sit close by, just in case he would harm himself or the kids. He was having frequent seizures, and he wouldn't recognize anyone during the outbreaks. I was the only one he could identify, he would refer to me as "Mom".

The last time I took him to have his monthly check-up, Dr. Noorbala, a psychiatrist and the head of the Veterans Psychiatry Department, told me the bitter truth.

"I wouldn't recommend that your husband stay at home anymore. I swear you and your children are in danger. It would be best to take him to a psychiatric facility, a psychological complex for psychiatric veterans. Admit him there. I assure you, it's better for him."

It was a bitter pill to swallow. It was as if they wanted to take my life away. Although he wasn't more than a pile of bones and skin, his looks were my love. He would speak through his looks, and they would warm my heart. His absence inflicted the same pain on me, as did his presence. I was thinking about the kids. They were so young. They too needed care. How much longer could my mom handle them? How much longer could I sit next to Hussein looking out for what he would do?" I admitted him to the facility. How could I fill his void in the house? It was burning me. I cried so profusely, that my parents decided to rent out their home and come and stay with us for a while.

In the beginning, I would visit him whenever I felt glum. I would go there after work, two or three times a week. I used to take the children along with me on Fridays. Although it was too short a time, they were extremely excited to spend that limited time with their father. Zeynab used to embroider on a tiny fabric with her small hands. She had sewn 'I love you' on it and once it was completed, she eagerly wrapped it as a gift for her father. They kept visiting with me for the next six or seven years. But they lost their enthusiasm to see that place. It was laden with psychiatric patients. The hospital gave the patients a couple of days leave, occasionally. I would bring him home on holidays or during Muharram.[39] I would take him out to see people mourning for Imam al-Husayn (a). I knew he loved Muharram. We used to go to *hei'at*[40] in the early days of Muharram when we were just married. It was near his mother's place. The

---

39. Muharram is the first month of lunar calendar during which the Shi'i Muslims mourn the tragedy of Husayn b. Ali (a) the Prophet's grandson.
40. *Hei'at* is a religious gathering to commemorate the Prophet's infallible household usually on their martyrdom or birth anniversaries.

upper floor was designated for women. They would cover the balcony there with a curtain. I would pull aside a corner of it, to see Hussein helping cook dinner. I reminisced about the days when Hussein was able to lift the heavy pots, for *nazri*.[41]

The psychiatric facility had its own problems. Hussein was residing in an eight-bed room. His roommates used to say, "Sometimes, when he's having seizures and falls from the bed, he shouts so much, until the staff comes to tend to him." I had no idea how they were actually treating him, but I would make complaints about their service each time. Once, they brought him home without any arrangements. I wasn't home, and I had locked the door, as I was running some errands. The kids were home alone and told them, "Our mom is not home, and she has locked the door." The hospital staff didn't buy that, though. They left Hussein behind the door, and the poor man stood behind the door for an hour. The kids watched him from the window,

---

41. *Nazri* food is a meal served for free by Shias on the anniversary of martyrdom or birth of infallible Imams, particularly during the days of Imam al-Husayn's (a) martyrdom.

but they couldn't do anything. Finally, the member of staff from the facility, standing a little further on the other side of the street, believed the kids and returned him to the hospital. Each time, his first couple of days at home would go smoothly, but everything would reoccur like the earlier days.

I had no choice but to lock the door. Once, I forgot to do so, and Hussein ran out of the house. I freaked out. My mom was not home, so I had a neighbor look after the kids and began looking for him in the streets. There was no sign of him. A police officer caught my eye. I gave him some information about Hussein, with a phone number and our address. I returned home and kept praying for his safety. At dusk, the police called us. "We found your husband near Keshavarz Boulevard. We will bring him back," they said. He sat down in the corner of the room, exhausted.

"Where did you go, Hussein? Why did you leave?" I asked him.

He calmly raised his head.

"I was feeling blue. I just wanted to go walking for a while."

He would cuddle the kids if he was in a good mood; otherwise, he would just sit somewhere having nothing to do with them. I would feel sorry for the kids, although I never complained about the circumstances. I would gather them around myself and talk to them. I would tell them in a childish language how precious it was to sacrifice what you like for God.

"Don't think your father has always been like this. You have no idea how patient, how kind, how good-looking and how brave he was back then."

I would show them some old photos of their father.

"Look, he was a fellow soldier of Dr. Chamran. He sacrificed his health for God, for us, and fought the enemies." I would tell them so much that they could feel it in their bones. I thought they were given divine strength, as they could bear that situation. Hussein would beat them sometimes, but they still wanted to hug him. They tasted their father's love with all their heart, although it was so brief. When Hussein was at the hospital, he used to call the kids five or six times a day, speaking to them and telling them how much he loved them. He would tell Zeynab, "My sweet girl. Talk to me. It refreshes me whenever you talk." When he was done talking to the kids, he would ask them to put me on the phone. Some days, the pain would prevent him from talking properly, but he would call home anyway, just to hear our voices. On the occasions when he was semi-conscious, he would assume the person behind the line was Zahra, no matter who would pick up the phone. It was the same before we took him to the facility. He would perceive everyone to be Zahra when he was ill, even Zeynab and Muhammad Hussein. Perhaps because she was his first child, he had experienced true fatherhood with her. His pain and illness never allowed him to experience the same feeling with his other two children.

I never wanted the kids to feel the absence of their father. So, when Zeynab once told me, on our way home from one of our friends' home, "Mom, if we had our dad with us, could we live in a big house like your friend's?" I told myself that I had to make our house larger for the kids, no matter what, but it was a demanding job. It was a tumbledown building, and its renovation was a headache. It also required a large sum of money, but it didn't matter, as it was what

Zeynab had wished for. Some architects and builders renovated the building, with one of our old family friends, Mr. Taheri, assisting us. I would send the kids to my brother's home at night, while my mom and I would sleep on a mattress on the metal beams.

The kids grew up and went to school. My mom used to do the daily chores, and tend to the kids, while I had a full-time job teaching in schools and institutions. Besides that, I used to hold private tutoring classes. I would get home at the kid's bedtime. I used to lie down with them, so they could cling to my hands, play with my fingers and talk to me in order to lift their gloom. I didn't want to seek charity. I knew Mom would sometimes put money in my purse, but she would deny it. I was preoccupied with the kids' future. When Zahra was accepted at Babol University, I said, "I won't let my daughter live in a dorm alone, without us." We packed our furniture and moved to Babol[42] with my mother. I could be at peace this way, but I could not afford to lose my job in Tehran. The school and private classes

---

42. Babol is a city in Mazandaran province, in the north of Iran, 220 km far from Tehran.

were my only source of income. So, I was on a constant commute between Babol and Tehran.

"You could at least leave for Tehran when I'm asleep. I don't want to see you leave. I get the blues when you leave," Zeynab told me once.

It set my heart on fire. I would leave home to get to the terminal at 2 a.m. every Tuesday to avoid being seen leaving. I used to take a cab to Tehran, but I couldn't afford to pay double to sit in the front seat. I had to take the back seat pushing myself against the door and window for several hours, to prevent touching the man sitting next to me, losing his balance in his sleep. I had to be in my classes at seven. I used to go visit Papa after school until Thursday when I returned to Babol. We stayed there for almost a year, until I managed to make Zahra's transfer to Khajeh Nasir University[43] happen.

I looked at the pointless patterns on the paper. Remembering Hussein's chiaroscuro

---

43. Khajeh Nasir al-Din Toosi University of Technology, also known as K. N. Toosi University of Technology, is a public research university located in Tehran.

would afflict my heart with pain. The staff was aware of his affection for drawing, and they provided him with some paper, a paintbrush, and watercolors. However, he would mostly scribble on those papers. They also had manual work, matting, for instance. If the results were of good quality, the hospital would host an exhibition and sell their products for them.

Hussein no longer had a proper sense of time. He would talk about things like they were happening at that moment, while they belonged to ten years prior. He could mostly recall memories prior to his injury. When he was made ward of the court for his mental disability, they said, "He should have a legal guardian." I was appointed as his guardian after a tiring paper chase.

I would smile whenever I visited him, concealing my pain under that smile. What good was unburdening myself? He couldn't do anything anyway, even if he could understand me when I poured myself out. It would just add to his burden of sorrows. Those days were exhausting, but I would feel the thrill of spending some time with him. I used to take him to the yard to walk next to him.

He used to give Zahra a piggyback ride. Zeynab and Muhammad Hussein hadn't been born then. We would go for a walk at night. One night, I wanted to catch his attention. "I feel like having an ice cream," I asked. He looked at me with surprise, "Right here in the street, Rani?"

"Yeah. Let's have it now. I mean, Zahra is craving for one."

"It's not the place to eat ice cream. I'll buy one for Zahra, but not for you."

"I'll have it under my *chador*. I will go home if you don't get me one."

"Alright, I will. At least let's go to that alley."

He bought two ice creams. He didn't have one. Zahra and I started to eat and giggle. I can still remember the taste.

My father passed away in September 2002. Hussein loved my father greatly, perhaps because he had lost his father early. I went to him after the funeral. I did not want to let him know of Papa's death and made a great effort to conceal my grief. We had an ordinary conversation, and he didn't find out anything that day. On the third day after

Papa's burial, the kids and I visited Hussein. He had gotten wind of something. someone might have informed him. The girls and I were wearing our *chadors*, so that he couldn't see our black clothing underneath. But Muhammad Hussein's black shirt revealed the truth. He started shouting.

"I'm such a terrible person. Too cowardly. Why shouldn't I be dead instead of him?"

"Hussein, what are you talking about? You think I would be here if Papa had died?"

He didn't fall for it.

"Swear to me Rani, that he's alive."

"He's alive, God-willing."

A while after Papa's death, I married Zahra off. Her husband, Hamed, was a nice boy. His brother was an MIA[44] soldier. I had been friends with his sister for a long time. We used to go to his mom's place when Zahra was still a child. We had broken bread; I could trust them. I was glad that

---

44. Missing in action (MIA) is a title assigned to combatants of war who are reported missing during wartime.

Zahra finally settled down. I told Hussein the story of the proposal meeting. After holding a private engagement ceremony, we went to the psychiatric facility. They did not allow Hussein to leave for the ceremony. He was sitting beneath a canopy in the yard. He took a look at Hamed. "Hussein, this is Hamed, our son-in-law," I said. Hamed stepped forward to shake hands and greet him. Hussein grabbed his hands and spoke to him.

"If you ever do anything to her, you're going to face me."

"What is this you're saying? It's your first meeting, for goodness' sake." I said.

I knew Hamed wouldn't get offended. I had explained everything to him beforehand. He was an understanding boy. Hussein still hadn't let go of his hands.

"Promise you won't hurt my daughter. Promise me."

Hamed responded with a kind smile.

"I promise you, Dad. I will make sure of it."

I had collected the dowry for Zahra through the years. You couldn't find anything missing. A few days after Papa's death anniversary, we booked a hall for their wedding. The day after the anniversary, I felt numbness in my hand, and my chest also felt heavy. The children called an ambulance. "It was a heart attack. You need to be hospitalized," they said. Hamed and Zahra were weeping.

"We'll call off the ceremony. We can postpone it to another time," Hamed said.

"For goodness' sake, don't. We will manage something by tomorrow," I said.

The doctor and nurses refused to let me leave for the wedding. No matter how many times I beseeched them.

"It's my daughter's wedding. Her father can't be there either. I must be beside her during the ceremony."

"It's too dangerous. A heart attack is no joke," they said.

The next day at 2 a.m., the medical staff changed shifts. I explained my situation to the new doctor, begging him for permission, for a couple of hours leave. I promised to return to the hospital. Finally, he gave his consent. I left the hospital at three, and headed home. I just changed my clothes and went to the hall. It was already one hour past the allocated time for the ceremony when I arrived there. We held the ceremony that night one way or another. They all did their best to take me back to the hospital the next day, but I disagreed. I told them I was feeling well. I couldn't stand that place.

Chapter 6

Final Promises

The hospital would not give Hussein leave for the last two years. We could only visit him there. He was diagnosed with hepatitis C and I didn't know that initially. The kids used to hug and kiss him as usual when we would pay him a visit, and I would also pat his head; until one day, a nurse called home.

"Mr. Shayesteh Far has been diagnosed with hepatitis C. Take care of your children. They are young, and we don't want them to get sick."

Hepatitis had damaged his liver. The only working kidney was now also lost. They transferred him to Sasan Hospital. He had to be on dialysis. First, they quarantined him in an isolated room. I would go to the hospital alone looking at him from behind the windows. But later, when they started dialyzing, I was able to approach him. He was on dialysis for two whole years. They had to place a shunt for him, a transparent tube placed between arteries and veins to circulate the fresh blood in the body.

They had tried a central venous catheter in all parts of his body. The last time, the doctor said, "He needs surgery. We should place the catheter in his head." They did the surgery without inducing anesthesia. I looked at him when he was finally out of the operation room. He was bare-boned, but he wouldn't whine. I went to him.

"Hussein, how are you feeling? Does it hurt?"

He calmly turned his head.

"Thank God. To be a man is to bear the pain."

He used to get up and sit when we visited him. But when he couldn't, he would just act fine. He would rub his head with a smile, like he was arranging his hair. I approached him to shake hands, as usual. But he suddenly grasped my hand to kiss it. I felt embarrassed in front of the kids. Hamed, my son-in-law, was also there. Hussein burst into tears. He kept on shedding tears.

"Why are you crying? You should not do that in front of the kids," I said.

"You must promise me something Rani. Promise me you won't look at anyone else after I die."

"What are you talking about? I devoted my youth to you."

He was crying.

"I swear to God, I won't come to see you anymore if you don't stop crying. Pull yourself together. What do you think of me?" I argued.

I called the hospital from my school. "He's not in his room," they said. I hadn't been able to visit him due to school-work pressure for a couple of days. I hung up. I called the hospital reception once more.

"Where is Shayesteh Far? Did you transfer him back to the psychiatric facility?"

"He has been taken to the ICU."

I hung up the phone and dashed to the hospital. I also told my mother and the kids to come. He went into a coma while having dialysis. Unlike the previous days, he did not sit or arrange his hair with laughter. We all approached his bed and greeted him, but he was lying down on the bed with no response, his eyes shut, completely senseless. I got closer.

"Hussein, it's me, Razieh."

Suddenly, he moved his hand. It was like he was trying to put all his strength to raise his hand. He was looking for my hand in the air. I had a hunch he would feel our presence, and hear our voices. I told the children, "Speak to your father. He is hearing you." They moved towards his bed one by one, bursting into tears. They talked to him and kissed him. On his turn, Muhammad Hussein stepped forward without crying. He was not even fifteen.

"Dad, it's Muhammad Hussein. I'll take care of Mom and my sisters. Don't worry about them," he said. He could not resist and burst into tears. Then he left the room.

After eighteen days, Hussein opened his eyes halfway. Without having any movement or reaction, he gazed at a point as if he was expecting something. I was unable to concentrate in my classes. Hussein's face with his eyes half-opened would cross my mind incessantly. "What if he still isn't confident about what I promised?" I rushed to the hospital immediately after school had finished.

"Don't be so unfair. So, it seems you never really got to know me. I give you my word of honor that I will not marry anyone after you. Who can fill your shoes?"

I was called from Sasan Hospital the next day at sunset. "The Bennett ventilator doesn't reach the bottom of his lungs. He needs a tracheotomy," they said. They had to make an incision in his throat to insert the tube into his lungs. They needed my permission, but I told them, "You know it isn't going to work. You'll only cause him pain for no good reason. Besides, you need his mother's permission. I'm not content with this." It had been a couple of years since I had appointed his mother as his guardian.

"Regardless, we are required to do whatever is necessary," the medical staff said. They called the Organization of Veterans and Martyrs, asking for Hussein's mother. They wanted her to go to the hospital for permission. She permitted it.

They performed the surgery that very night. I didn't visit him the next day. I could not bear this one.

I was unable to sleep for two nights, staying awake the whole time. I could barely mount the stairs on Thursday. I felt like my heart was going to stop working. Anyhow, I got to my class and had just started to teach when my cell phone rang. It was my mom. She stayed home with Muhammad Hussein and Zeynab. She never used to call me during my classes; I felt butterflies in my stomach. I answered the call.

"Can you get back home, Razieh?"

"I can't right now. My class will finish at 12:30 p.m. What's wrong?"

"You should get back home right now."

"For goodness' sake, Mom. What happened?"

She grew silent for a moment.

"Verily we belong to Allah and verily to Him do we return,"[45] she finally uttered.

The phone dropped to the ground.

---

45. An Islamic phrase expressed when someone dies, taken from Quran 2:156.

When I opened my eyes, the school staff were around me. They had removed my headscarf and splashed some water on my face. I didn't want to believe it. I pulled myself together. "Mrs. Jafari, please call the hospital. They've already told me 'Your husband is about to die, come and say your farewell,' several times. That might be the case, again," I told the assistant principal. She called Sasan Hospital and asked about Hussein. They inquired who she was, and how they were related. When they figured out that she was a friend of mine, they told her, "Unfortunately, he passed away last night."

It was all over. He was finally unfettered from the pain and agony. Now, I was all alone with the anguish of not having him anymore. I got back home to take his documentation in order to discharge his body from the hospital. I called Zeynab's school consultant to prepare her for the sad news. She was more emotionally attached to her father than the other children. I was worried that she couldn't bear the heart-breaking news of her father's death. I was awake throughout the night thinking, "Now it's my turn to make him promise me. What should I ask him for our hereafter, now that his body is departing this mundane world forever?"

The next day, a massive crowd of friends and neighbors gathered before our door, along with the IRGC authorities. Mr. Taheri had a private ambulance bring Hussein's body to our home and rented a few buses to take the mourning crowd to the cemetery. One of our neighbors was a eulogist. When they brought Hussein home, the mourners recited Ziyarat Ashura[46] and beat their chests.[47] A frenzy of sorrow prevailed over the alley. We set off for the cemetery along with five or six buses and some private vehicles. Some other relatives and friends came from Hussein's mother's house. In the graveyard, people joined us in

---

46. Ziyarat Ashura is a salutatory supplication addressed to Imam al-Husayn (a), the third Shiite Imam, which is recommended to be recited, particularly on the Day of Ashura the day on which Imam al-Husayn (a) was martyred.

47. *Sinazani* or chest-beating is a traditional ritual of Shiite mourning ceremonies, in which a *maddah* (eulogist) recites a poem with a certain rhythm, and mourners beat their chests in harmony with the eulogy. Famously, the practice is inherited from the mourning practice of Arab women in the early Islamic centuries.

salat al-janazah,[48] upon finding out Hussein was a martyr. Multiple people lined up for prayer. I was on the verge of tears when they finished praying. I thought to myself, *look, you can't get close enough to talk to him. Not even now.* I could barely see him, as a massive crowd was standing ahead of me. He was taken a hundred-meters further on their hands in the blink of an eye. I dashed into the crowd, but still, I couldn't reach his coffin. I was bursting into tears, when suddenly someone shouted.

"Let his children pass. They haven't said farewell to their father yet."

Perhaps, it was my brother, or maybe my brother-in-law. I don't know who they were; I just wished blessings upon them. Then, the crowd parted, and my daughters and I reached Hussein's body. They covered his coffin with a large flag and a wreath. Muhammad Hussein was sitting next to him. I put my *chador* on Hussein's head and mine and whispered in his ears. I didn't want anyone to hear me, not even our children.

---

48. The funeral prayer or *salat al-janazah* is an obligatory prayer that should be said on the corpse of a Muslim.

"Hussein, I know you are hearing me. I don't want to bother you much, but I want you to promise me a thing or two. I suffered a lot living with you. You didn't notice most of that. I'm not here to make complaints, but I wish for you to make me two promises. First, you are a descendant of Lady Zahra (a) and Imam Ali (a). Ask them for my intercession, the kids, and my mother's. I know you can do this. The second one is that you stay beside me forever. You couldn't do that because of your pain when you were here. I was always alone, but now I hope you can make me feel your presence everywhere I go, so I can be confident that my husband has my back. Now, you need to come in my dreams in any way possible and make these two promises. Don't you dare try to answer me through other people's dreams; only mine, so I can be rest assured; or I will not talk to you anymore, not even on the Day of Judgment."

Everyone assumed I was weeping. But I was pouring out what I had confined for so long. A woman got close to me and whispered in my ears.

"Ma'am, get up. It's enough. He's a martyr. He belongs to all of us."

I raised my head, annoyed.

"I'm not finished yet. You have no idea how much is left unsaid. I won't get up until I'm done talking."

Once more, I put my mouth close to his ear.

"Hussein! I ask you one more thing. Don't let the *houries*[49] make you forget me. Forget about me if you ever go after them."

I recalled one of my friends whose husband was also a martyr once said, "They'll go after their pleasures, and we are left alone with their grief."

"Hussein, I will have nothing to do with you if you ever forget about me, even for a moment. I want you to promise the same thing you made me promise."

My brother came next to me.

"Razieh, get up. Don't keep the people waiting."

I felt slightly relieved. They put him in the grave. I had brought a sack with me, filled with items from the sacred soil

---

49. *Hour al-Ayn* or *houri* is the beautiful heavenly virgin whose description is given in the Quran and will be the companion of believing men in heaven.

of the Pure Five[50] including an agate ring with their names carved on, blessed green fabric, and water taken from the Zamzam Well.[51] Zahra's brother-in-law stepped into the grave to perform *talqin al-mayyit*,[52] and I handed him the items one by one. They covered his grave with soil. I sat down next to the grave to recite the Quran. A crowd of mourners gathered around me. I heard them talking.

"I pity him. His wife had left him for the last few years," said the woman next to me.

It set my heart on fire. I looked at her.

"Ma'am, how are you related to him?" I asked.

"I'm his mother's neighbor. I heard his wife had abandoned him."

"I'm his wife. According to both law and

---

50. The Pure Five is a title for the Prophet (s), Imam Ali (a), Lady Fatima (a), Imam al-Hasan (a) and Imam al-Husayn (a), whose common virtues and positions distinguish them from other Infallibles (a).
51. Zamzam Well is a sacred well located within the Masjid al-Haram in Mecca.
52. *Talqin al-mayyit* is a recommended part of burying a corpse, according to Islamic jurisprudence.

Shariah. Do you want me to show you my identification? Why do you spoil your faith in God for nothing?"

She apologized.

"I forgive you! But how many other people have you told this to? How many others will they tell? May God grant us all his mercy," I said.

I was aware of the gossip around us, but I would cheer myself up with my ever-inflamed love for Hussein.

Our modest home hosted a multitude of people that night, including my friends, official figures, their wives, and many others. Many men and women we had met in the two mosques of Lady Zaynab (a) in Sina Street, and the one in our neighborhood where Muhammad Hussein used to be a member of its Basij and its cultural office, would bring solace to our grieving family. They set up speakers and performed a mourning ceremony. I didn't cry. I never liked to weep at any funeral in public, not even in one of my dearest ones. Zeynab and Zahra were also being patient. I knew they were choking back their tears for my sake.

One of my friends fell into my arms at once, wailing. Her shrieking noise echoed in my ears. My heart grew heavy, abruptly. I had already survived two cardiac arrests, so my heart wasn't strong. I fell to the ground. They called an ambulance, and the paramedics came upstairs. I sank into the chair, feeling lethargic. They couldn't mover the stretcher, as the staircase was too narrow for them to pass. One of the paramedics was my college friend back at Shahid Beheshti University. He recognized me.

"Mrs. Bobash, I'm so-and-so. Do you remember me?" He kept asking persistently.

I couldn't remember him.

"Don't move her at all," he asked.

He grabbed the chair leg asking Muhammad Hussein, Hamed, and my brother to hold the others. They took me downstairs on that very chair. They laid me down on a stretcher, and we left for the hospital in an ambulance. On the fourth night of insomnia, my sisters and my sister-in-law, along with some of my friends came to visit me in the hospital.

"Only one accompanying person is allowed," the doctor uttered.

Hamed stayed. I felt as if my head was boiling. My eyes were burning, but I was not able to fall asleep.

"Call the nurse to inject a shot of diazepam as I am having difficulty sleeping," I asked Hamed. It was not until 4 a.m. that my eyes got heavy. I saw Hussein approaching me. He stroked and cuddled me.

"Rani, you can be rest assured. I'll fulfill the promises," he said, embracing me.

"Hussein, these are big promises to make. Are you sure you can keep them?"

"I told you already. Rest assured."

My headache faded away as I opened my eyes. Hamed was standing beside me.

"Mom, are you alright? It seems you fell asleep for ten minutes," he said.

However, to me, it passed like a couple of hours. I had to stay in the hospital for a few more days.

Hussein's family held the third-day funeral ceremony. And I was planning to hold the fifth-day one. Family and friends came from far and wide to attend the ceremony; however, the physicians refused to discharge me.

"You mustn't move a muscle. Bedrest only", they said.

One day prior to the ceremony, I hosted a multitude of visitors in my room.

"Make them grant me leave for God's sake, brother. I beg you. How am I supposed to miss my own husband's post-funeral gathering?" I implored my brother. He was not willing to do so.

"It'll make you feel worse. It doesn't matter if you are not there, your children will be there," he retorted.

No matter how hard I tried to impress the nurses to get a one-day leave, they still rejected my request.

"One of your relatives, either your mother or your children, needs to sign a certificate of consent," they told me.

"Please sign the paper. What can go wrong?" I beseeched Zahra.

She was in a quandary, but she gave up, eventually. My brother became frustrated. "Getting leave doesn't mean you can come to the mosque. Stay home. You'll meet the guests there," he said. I crawled up the stairs. Muhammad Hussein had arranged almost everything by himself. He had distributed the obituary notice in all the neighboring districts, as well as the schools I had worked for. He had purchased fruit and booked the mosque without anyone urging him to do so. I was realizing what 'like father like son' could mean.

I would dream about Hussein almost every time I fell asleep. That night was no exception. He sat next to me and talked with deep affection.

"Put some cotton in your ears before going to the mosque," he said with laughter. He kissed my cheek and left. I thought deeply about what he said. I thought it might have been for the emotional atmosphere in the mosque. He must have suggested that so I wouldn't fall ill again.

My brother arrived home just before the beginning of the ceremony, as I was getting prepared to go to the mosque.

"You promised me, Razieh!"

"I can't keep it up, Ali. I swear to God I'll act prudently. Look, I even put cotton in my ears to avoid irritation."

He agreed somewhat reluctantly. While I was in the mosque, my mom, Zahra, and

Mrs. Jafari watched over me. I saw one of our relatives approach Zeynab murmuring in her ears in the ceremony's final moments. Zeynab frowned. It was one of those hackneyed gossips.

"You left the poor man in a psychiatric facility, so that you can live in peace," they used to say.

Whatever they would tell me seemed to go in one ear and out the other. Then I realized why Hussein recommended putting cotton in my ears.

My brother intended to take me back to the hospital after the ceremony.

"I swear to God, I'll die in that hospital," I said.

"Then you have to stay upstairs and rest."

I agreed. The only matter of delight in my life was sleeping and dreaming about Hussein.

Hussein kept his word. He always accompanies me. He often informs me by some means or other, of significant events beforehand. His presence warms my soul. I even sometimes feel the air filled with his scent. I kept myself busy studying, in an effort to deal with the absence of his body beside me. Zahra enrolled me in the MA courses at Islamic Azad University. She knew I liked Arabic literature. In April, not more than two months after Hussein's martyrdom, she advised me.

"Mom, you should take the entrance exam."

"No way. I've forgotten what I have learned. I can't concentrate."

She disagreed. She took me to the exam center, as though I was a school kid. She loitered behind the door until I was finished. Sometime later, the children returned home holding a newspaper, the news of the university acceptance.

Every Friday, I would pray *salat* after *fajr adhan*,[53] and I used to go to Behesht-e Zahra;[54] in summer or winter, under the rain

---

53. *Adhan* is a call for Muslims, which informs them of the time of prayer
54. Behesht-e Zahra is Tehran's largest cemetery, where many martyrs of the Islamic Revolution, martyrs of the Iraqi war on Iran, and many other Iranian political and religious figures are buried.

or snow. On Fridays, I would be at Hussein's grave, come hell or high water. It would invigorate me to keep on living.

When Zahra's daughter was about to be born, I dreamed about Hussein treating me with some pastry, with a big smile on his face. Zahra called me on November 8, 2007.

"Mom, I need to go to the hospital. I think it's time."

November 8th was Hussein's birthday. Zahra's daughter was supposed to be born in December, but apparently, she intended to brighten up our hearts on her grandfather's birthday.

"You and Hamed hurry to the hospital. Zeynab and I will be there soon."

I called the hospital in which Zahra was supposed to deliver. I was acquainted with the nurses and physicians there. I put in a good word for Zahra, so that they would treat her with utmost care. We were all apprehensive about the delivery. She was transferred to the surgery room, and a few hours later, the baby was born.

We named the baby girl "Narges," the same name Hussein wished for his daughters.

I embraced Hussein's granddaughter on his birthday. I looked at her tiny face. I think of the life that is continuing after Hussein, of the hope and love that never ceases; but remains, with the same passion, the same warmth, and divine as ever. And now, I am more confident than ever, that "There is no regret in making bargains with God."